Quirky

A Humorous Peek at Our Animal Friends and Ourselves

TIM HARSHMAN

Illustrations by Lyon Ganun

Copyright © 2023 Tim Harshman
All rights reserved
First Edition

NEWMAN SPRINGS PUBLISHING
320 Broad Street
Red Bank, NJ 07701

First originally published by Newman Springs Publishing 2023

ISBN 979-8-88763-376-3 (Paperback)
ISBN 979-8-88763-370-1 (Digital)

Printed in the United States of America

To Mary L.

Foreword

As humans, we have been blessed to coexist on our planet earth with millions of very different, spectacular animals and insect species.

Maybe in this existence, we humans are considered top dog, but there is a great deal we can learn about nature and ourselves from our animal friends.

Just for laughs, what if in this symbiotic relationship, animals were more like humans? Some may say, "Heaven forbid," but the quirkiness of that combination lends itself to a lot of smiles, grins, giggles, and laughs if you let yourself think outside the box. Hope you enjoy looking at yourselves and our animal friends in a new light.

Quirkies

1. The sticky-tongued lizard walked into his favorite greasy spoon and ordered the Tuesday special. When the waitress placed the order in front of him, what did she ask?

   Answer: Do you want ketchup with your flies?

2. How can you tell if an opossum is really dead or just playing dead?

   Answer: Just tickle the bottoms of their feet.

3. Do most amoebas have only one cell phone?

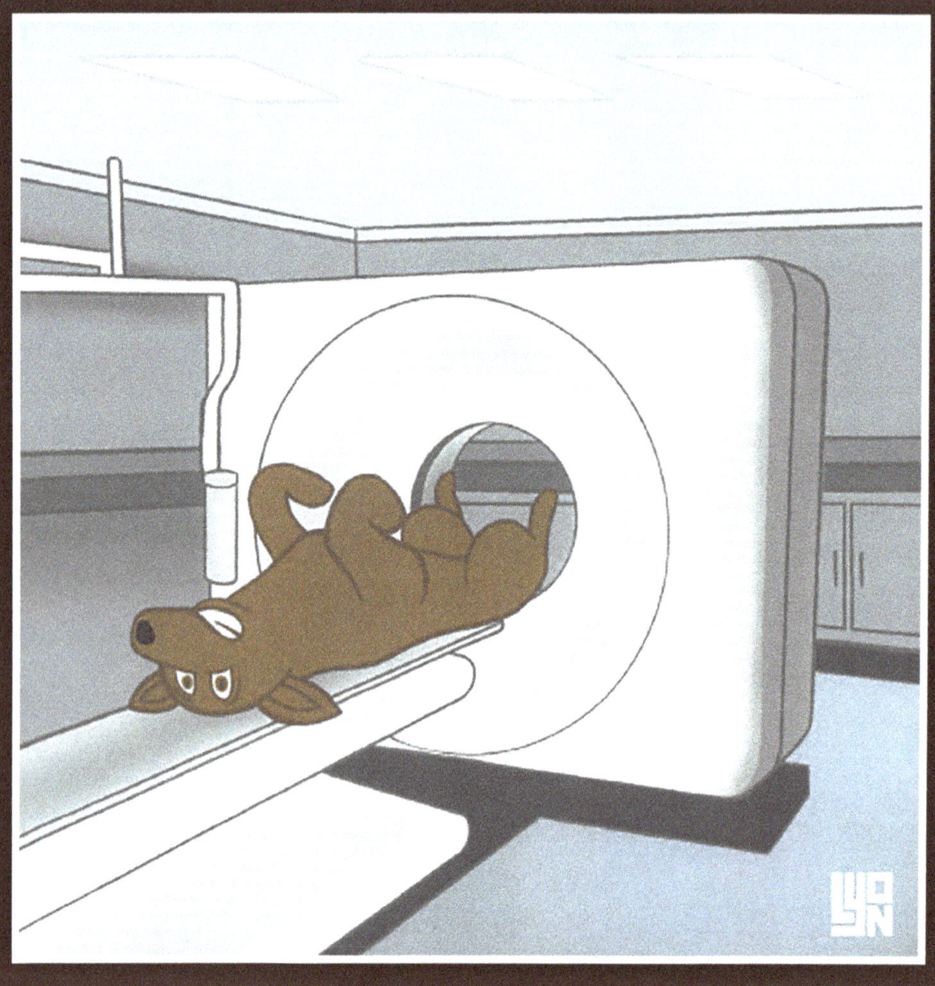

What diagnostic equipment do
veterinarians often use?

Answer: PET scan.

4. When a dairy farmer goes to the gym, does he often think of his calves?

5. What do you call a pika that has had a sex change?

Answer: A turn pika.

6. The dancing troop of sheep had to perform after probably the best singer in the *America's Got Talent* competition. What was the troop leader's main concern?

Answer: Even for sheep, she was a tough act to follow.

Why was the father spider so
much taller than his offspring?

Answer: The daddy had long legs.

7.   Is the very end of a cottonmouth called a cottontail?

8.   Did nature plan it this way, or is the blue whale's tail a fluke?

9.   Does a male anaconda have a main squeeze?

10.   At the underwater circus, which act got the most laughs?

      Answer: The three hundred clownfish piling out of the tiny Volkswagen.

11.   Are all French poodles intense kissers?

If the FBI hides a listening device
in a suspect's mattress, does that
device become a bed bug?

12. Eight-year-old Sammy loved two things: his two Louisville sluggers and his town's unique clock tower. When spring practice rolled around, Sammy couldn't find his sluggers—then it dawned on him. He may have left them in the clock tower on his last visit. He ran to the tower. What did he find?

Answer: His bats were in the belfry.

13. If a mating pair of loons have an offspring, is that baby considered a little loony?

14. When thinking of their family, do most male lions have a sense of pride?

What wild cat is known to love
spending time on a golf course?

Answer: The lynx.

15. Chester the pig had worked at the meatpacking company for six years. At Christmas, the company gave their employees a bonus. The employee could choose one cut of any meat to take home. What would Chester choose?

Answer: You could always count on Chester to bring home the bacon.

16. Who was the daughter of the commercial fisherman that discovered a herring-like fish could be eaten as a relish or pizza topping?

Answer: Ann Chovy.

Don't you feel empathy for an
animal who is trying to defecate
when its yucky is stucky?

17. When a pony has a sore throat, does he feel a little horse?

18. Do turkeys believe in gobble warming?

19. When driving their cars, do politically conservative ornithologists only make right terns?

20. Do boll weevils often drink too much cotton gin?

21. Before a pig begins his intense workout in the gym, does he stretch his hamstrings?

22. For insects, what is the highlight of their busy social season?

Answer: The mothball.

If a canine takes a trip to the sauna,
does that make him a hot dog?

23. If a mother hen is afraid to defend her chicks from an attacking fox, will the other hens call her a *chicken*?

24. In Hong Kong, ponies pulled carts for human transportation until it became too unsanitary. Who was the first actual person to pull a cart for other individual riders?

Answer: Rick Shaw.

25. If two crabs get divorced, might one of them end up paying abalone?

26. If a male lion had a sex change, would he no longer be a mane squeeze?

27. For some reason, every time the silverback lifted the heavy weight above his head, he thought of his old girlfriend Barb Bell.

28. It's a little-known fact that the daughter of Atticus in the movie *To Kill a Mockingbird* was an avid bird lover. So avid, she dyed her hair blonde so her friends would call her by the name of her favorite species. What was that name?

Answer: Gold Finch

29. What favorite aquarium fish is sold by the ounce?

Answer: The goldfish.

30. If a night crawler spent all night reading, would he become a bookworm?

31. Because his friends couldn't go, the young crow decided to go to the horror movie by himself. As the movie progressed, he became more and more anxious. Eventually he got up and ran out of the theater. Why did he leave?

Answer: He was one scared crow.

32. The farm agent made a serious mistake when typing the announcement for the beginning of the pheasant hunting season. It's now OK to hunt peasants starting November 10.

33. If two buffalos mate and have a male offspring, is that calf a bi-son?

34. Did Old McDonald sell quarter pounders down on his farm?

35. Why don't you ever want to eat those birds that return to Capistrano each year?

   Answer: Because they are hard to swallow.

36. In football terms, a blitzer is usually a linebacker who charges the offensive line when the ball is snapped. In lupine terms, if a wolf played linebacker, what would he be called?

   Answer: A wolf blitzer.

37. The only bird that can fly backwards is the hummingbird. How can it use this ability to its advantage?

Answer: When it loses its wallet, it can easily retrace its steps.

38. Does an anteater have nieces and nephews?

39. What bird is often found perched atop the entrance to an outhouse?

Answer: A stool pigeon.

40. Why do so many poisonous snakes think of their leader as a cool customer?

Answer: He never seems to get rattled.

41. Who was the jockey whose mount was within ten lengths of winning the derby, but suddenly pulled up lame because of a debilitating muscle cramp?

Answer: Charlie Horse.

42. What animal has the worst reputation for two-timing his mate?

Answer: A cheat-ah.

43. Year after year, the old bull had to defend his herd dominance from young challengers. After this last cycle, he had had enough. He needed a change. Why did he move on?

Answer: He was in a rut.

44. Why do few chorus directors choose the flounder to sing with their choir?

Answer: Because their singing is often flat.

45. What is the perfect animal to run errands in a large corporate office?

Answer: A gopher.

46. What reptile eats mostly Waldorf, Chef, and tossed salads?

Answer: The salad-mander.

What does the bald eagle think when
he takes a look in the mirror?

Answer: Maybe I should try Rogaine…

47. If a common housefly is trapped in the soft margarine on your kitchen countertop, will it eventually become a butterfly?

48. If the parents of a newborn male goat would name him William, would his friends call him Billy Goat?

49. The corporation's bank of computers suddenly went haywire. Something had infected the main terminal. What could be causing so much disruption?

Answer: A little mouse had gone berserk.

Why might you not want to hire
a flamingo as an attorney?

Answer: He only has one leg to stand on.

50. Why don't you ever want to eat a chicken that has been raised in a contaminated environment?

Answer: Because it tastes foul.

51. So many beautiful islands dotted the coastline that authorities numbered them instead of naming each. One of the islands was littered and unkempt. It was going to the dogs. Which one?

Answer: Cay nine.

52. If Paul, Ringo, John, and George had come from the Land of the Rising Sun, would they have been Japanese beetles?

Technically speaking, would it be considered a biracial marriage if a black mamba married a white elephant?

53. Arthur and Ben were twin rabbits. Arthur moved away, and Ben heard that his brother was having joint inflammation problems. Ben wrote to his brother. What did he say?

Answer: Art-write-us.

54. The mountain goats considered most of their distant cousins real bores. They didn't have much personality or sense of humor. They never wanted to play any games or have any fun. Who were these stuffy cousins?

Answer: They were from the dull sheep side of the family.

55. Has anyone ever taken a kangaroo to court?

If a finned fish learns to drive an armored vehicle, can it have its own TV show?

Answer: Yes, *Shark Tank.*

56. What fish has an intense need to hang out with other fish of his/her species?

Answer: The grouper.

57. The kingfisher's cousin had a malfunctioning trumpet that had to be repaired. What did the cousin get when he picked up the instrument from the repair shop?

Answer: A hornbill.

58. Do you need four quarter horses to have one complete horse?

59. What do you have to do when your pet baby skunk has an unpleasant odor?

Answer: Change its diaper.

Does a yellow jacket ever
think of changing coats?

60. Do jellyfish like peanut butter sandwiches?

61. Is the beaver held in such high esteem by his fellow pond residents because he gives a dam?

62. What mischievous ocean creature found numerous ways to trick almost any fisherman and steal their bait?

Answer: A sea urchin.

63. What expensive sports car do wealthy sheep dogs drive?

Answer: A Lam-borghini.

64. Are hyenas easily amused?

65. The HGTV producers made a huge mistake when they announced the wrong winner of their beautiful model home giveaway. Where were they now?

Answer: In their newly remodeled doghouse.

66. How can you tell if a snake is about to strike?

Answer: You have to look closely to see if it is carrying a union picket sign.

67. Does a Holstein ever go steer crazy?

68. In a porcupine's living room, what are you most likely to find on their sofa?

Answer: Pin cushions.

69. What animal is persistently and tediously complaining about how climate change is causing its food supply to disappear?

Answer: The harp seal.

70. Do skunks use deodorant?

71. What reptiles can often be found hiding under employee lockers in many Costco, Walmart, or Home Depot stores?

Answer: Box turtles.

72. When a pachyderm is on his computer and has to select a certain size print for his document, which one does he usually choose?

Answer: The ella font.

73. If a bear goes six months without shaving, does his beard become grizzly?

74. Why did the rooster refuse the raise in salary offered by his employer?

Answer: He thought it was chicken feed.

75. Do most minks wear a coat during the winter?

76. Do skylarks prefer to drive Buicks?

77. The altruistic river dweller always wanted to help others. After finishing his lengthy education, what did he become?

Answer: A skilled sturgeon.

78. As the vacationers walked the beach along the Atlantic coast, they observed, out in the water, a mahi-mahi struggling to make any headway. What was its problem?

Answer: It had a dull fin.

79. Does a collie ever get melancholy?

80. When a hyena hears a really funny joke, could he possibly die laughing?

81. What bird can you spend hours shooting and then mold their remains into a vase?

Answer: A clay pigeon.

82. Two weeks ago, the owner of the shoe store had her mother dog give birth to eight little ones in the storeroom. When the little ones would get too noisy the owner would stick her head in. What would she say?

Answer: "Hush, puppies."

83. What was the reply of the elephant of Italian descent when asked why he traveled to Alabama to see a bone specialist?

Reply: "My tusk-a-lose-a."

84. Do most Catholics think of the cardinal as a bird of pray?

When parked on a lover's lane,
what activity might you find
giraffes engaging in?

Answer: Necking.

85. Twelve-year-old Rebecca was so excited when her dad said she could go with him on a deep-sea fishing trip that she yelled out an expression of glee. What was that expression?

Answer: "Wahoo!"

86. The aquarium principal was so tired of disciplining students who had been sent to the office that she wished for the impossible. What was that wish?

Answer: A school of angelfish.

87. Whatever happened to the fish that played the shark in the hit movie *Jaws*?

Answer: It became a famous starfish.

Why does it always seem that
you find dogs and cats hiding
during a thunderstorm?

Answer: Because they are pet-rified.

88. What is the most educated mammal in the ocean?

Answer: The humpback of Notre Dame.

89. The fishing pond on the church grounds hadn't been stocked in three years, it needed to be replenished. What fish was most numerous in the restocking?

Answer: The soul.

90. The bluefin must have been lost. It was swimming dangerously near the outdated coal burning power plant. What could happen if it got too close to the heated discharged waters?

Answer: It would become a tuna melt.

91. Do female deer who do the same work as male deer earn less doe?

Why shouldn't a bank manager ever
hire a gray tree frog as a teller?

Answer: Because he has sticky fingers.

92. What primate from India is often used in research to study the effects of the combination of peanut butter and chocolate on human beings?

Answer: The Reese's monkey.

93. Why don't you want an aardvark for a next-door neighbor?

Answer: They are always sticking their nose in your business and trying to dig up dirt on you.

94. The fur trapper wasn't sure what was in his snare, was it a beaver or a muskrat? What did he decide?

Answer: It was one or the otter.

95. When huskies finish their Iditarod run, what condition are they in?

Answer: Dog tired.

96. How did the four-winged nectar gathering insect react when it heard there was a sale on pollen at the shopping center?

Answer: It made a beeline to the mall.

97. What did the girl's parents think of her new boyfriend who was stingy with the condiments at the zoo sponsored BBQ?

Answer: He didn't pass mustard.

98. The ocean freighter, carrying a strong cleaning chemical, had run aground and was leaking a large amount of that agent. Unfortunately, the largest mammal in the ocean swam directly into the contaminated area. What was the result?

Answer: A bleached whale.

99. It was a small regional park that only employed five people, but when budget restraints hit, the staff was reduced to only one employee. Who was that one employee?

Answer: It was the lone ranger.

100. If dogs could go ocean cruising, like we humans do, then maybe there could be a TV show about their adventures. What would the show possibly be called?

Answer: The Unconditional Love Boat.

Other works by the author: *A Punny for Your Thoughts* and *A Punny for Your Thoughts 2*